Croquet Lover at the Dinner Table

For Tom

Croquet Lover at the Dinner Table/ Poems by Jonathan Aldrich

A Breakthrough Book/ University of Missouri Press
Columbia & London, 1977

University of Missouri Press
Library of Congress Catalog Card Number 76–45630
Printed and bound in the United States of America

Library of Congress Cataloging in Publication Data

Aldrich, Jonathan, 1936–
    Croquet lover at the dinner table.

    (A Breakthrough book)
    I. Title.
PS3551.L342C7   811'.5'4   76–45630
ISBN 0–8262–0205–5

Grateful acknowledgment is made to editors of the following magazines, in which the following poems first appeared:
American Weave (the poem was also printed in a pamphlet by the Academy of American Poets): "Croquet Lover at the Dinner Table"; *Approaches*: "Ars Poetica," "Rondo," "Tiger Lilies," "Before the Prophet"; *The Beloit Poetry Journal*: "Loss of the Unicorn," "Walking Home" (originally "Young Shakeresses Walking Home"); *Buffalo*: "Two in the Oak"; *The Chicago Review*: "Winter Fantasy"; *Inlet*: "Fable"; *The Kentucky Poetry Review*: "Bread"; *Lucille*: "Country Matters," "Postscript," "Suite"; *The Massachusetts Review*: "To a Young Lady at the Museum"; *Mitre Press* (England): "Van Gogh: 'Starry Night'"; *Quarry* (Canada): "Genesis," "The Millennial Laws," "Half-Song"; *Quartet*: "Tradewinds" (originally "Homage to Shakers"); *The Southern Poetry Review*: "Marks: after Edward Thomas"; *Triad*: "Note on Henry VIII"; *Twigs*: "The Glassblower," "Bells"; *West Coast Poetry Review*: "A Romantic Angel" (originally "A Separate Angel"), "At Home"; *Wisconsin Poetry Magazine*: "Willow Street."

Contents

One: "For each friend . . ."

Leaving, 8
Fading Blues, 9
Now Sun, 15
November, 16
Winter Fantasy, 18
Rondo, 19
Van Gogh: "Starry Night," 20

Bells, 21
Notes, 22
Suite, 23
Fable, 24
Bread, 25
Postscript, 26

Two: Shaker Village

The Girl, 29
   i: Genesis, 30
  ii: The Millennial Laws, 31
 iii: Half-Song, 32
  iv: Walking Home, 33
The Boy, 35
   i: Shadow Box, 36

  ii: Fruitlands, 37
 iii: Changeling: Child and
      the World, 38
  iv: Asthma, 39
   v: Two in the Oak, 40
  vi: In Time of Harvest, 41
 vii: Tiger Lilies, 42
viii: Tradewinds, 43

Three: "She passes muffins . . ."

Croquet Lover at the Dinner Table, 46
Passion of Crows, 47
Slow Motion, 48
Loss of the Unicorn, 49
Before the Prophet, 50
Marks, 53
The Glassblower, 54
Note on Henry VIII, 55

To a Young Lady at the Museum, 56
A Romantic Angel, 57
Country Matters, 58
Jumping, 59
At Home, 62
Willow Street, 63
Ars Poetica, 64

ONE:
"For each friend . . ."

Leaving

After a little time
away, he stopped for gas
beside a funeral home.
It seemed peculiarly close.

For each friend a stone.
A willowy one for Nan,
for Art the florid one,
a little fat one for Jane.

Some others, too, of lime,
marble, and alabaster—
and one that wore a name,
and his heart went faster.

Fading Blues

a.

Warm night alone,
I stare
again at my dusty
two-bulb chandelier,

a Holmes without his
Watson. Just burned in
on the wind's roulette,
below my screen

a sidekick June bug is
playing her cards right,
and her singing leg
tonight

floats over my thin
scholarship and library,
to admit herself
like me, a solitary.

I too am essentially
mobile and cannot help
answering almost any
appeal for help,

and appreciate her
stopping to send up
a low-down song from her crucible,
and carry me to sleep.

b.

I was called in over pearls,
a small matter of blackmail.

Good! The capital sky
was a pastel blue; his aqua
pool, a trapezoidal inset, lay
out in forsythia deck chairs,
a short springboard at the deep end;
the spicy box trees sat
like wrappers around palms that went straight up
and drooped leaves. Already
spring had peaked, the way
the Renaissance came early to Italy.
And the valet passing hors d'oeuvres,
he was a rare old coin.

My client White, after his business
weekend south, was mixing
martinis with twists,
the afternoon comfortably opening up
despite the robbery,
when I spotted,
                below the fretted
water, a deeper deposit,
a body hunched and doubled down.

As together we forked
her up, her mouth and nostrils
beading a rosary, her hair
and limbs without interest swinging
the way, in bathwater, your genitals
swing like a leaf,

it came clear to me that others soon
might have to be roughed up around here,
if they didn't sing.

c.

For my client White
his rake-off life
and smoking Little Productos
seemed to accrue—

until, of course, the blackmail
notes, and now
this trouble with his pool.

Unlucky ordeal,
his partner's wife
sunk in the pool,
and the fellow running off!

But when there are hot
jewels loose
or floating about,
the underworld wants a piece.

d.

Murder! murder! for days a deathpiece
ticked away, like the click of a die
in his skullbone, or a snake eye

rolling her endless ways: her amazed
comic-book smile, her warm love for God,
her casseroles. How when she sneezed
she went repeatedly "achoo-achoo"
as if she had read it. Love, she would do
it only on her back, with certainly
no success of angels, while her ring flared,
the snake nibbling its tail, eternity.

Murder! murder! faster a deathpiece played
its ugly tune out to the final toss.
He sank her in White's pool, and fled.

e.

This harbor sky today could hardly
be emptier if I said nothing.

f.

The killer's gone, his hurried feet
left nothing in the sand . . .
☞ Fade to White's balcony, where we sit
for nightcaps over the drained
pool. A first leg of the stars
comes out.

And doesn't comfort him.
Hearing surf on the empty sandbeach
down where his debonair estate
ends, he is drowsing off.
Well, I'm just hungry enough
myself to keep this case, trying to clear his name—
though I can see his fate,

someday kaput the Market
and the Exchange, someday the dollar
floating and coins floating out of his pocket,
his manhood and wristwatch
whirled on the waves away,

a new world rolling in deeper
nearer sleep—but me,
oh, I'd like it there,
I'd like it more and more.

Now Sun

Now sun goes under wood,
my ghostly father garlanded,
now sun goes under tree,
my ghostly father, sing for me.

November

Lifting his head from her thighs
he finds a little snow falling
vertically, first of the year,
history unwinding.
                    And sees,
seeding the air, unlikely
impediments and dyestuff,
pretty enough when there's
a rhythm going for you
1,000 feet above
sea level—and the morning
air is so numinous
life hungers for itself,
itself again, and joy
has risen to this room
that easy lovers keep.
But what is that quickening fringe
of air doing so early
and gentle out there, before
breakfast? And when a war's
newspaper faces stare
at you, where will disgrace
come from, and where will grace?
unless it is the snow
falling to intercept
a watery shoreline, moving
as tentative in and out,
softly it falls somewhere
irenic, the gauzy, headlong
edge of the snow, as off,
snow on the polar penguins
falls, and tightens
the melting polar cap
and the drifting continents,

as it falls more faintly
homeward,
                across day's quaint
geography, her legs
lie open like a wishbone,
and the sun arriving, abrupt.

Winter Fantasy

This for my-lady's neckpiece:—
they have let the red fox go,
and the bell on his collar
tinkles out of the morning, over the snow.

Picture five hunters riding
brown horses with black tails who, at a horn,
turn from the center of the morning
into the yellow sun

(one hunter remembering hills of the home
he cursed), the low hounds nosing ahead
where the fox has clipped the bright crust, his track
a skitter of beads;

and a faraway sled
glides down a hill, its trail
curved like an elephant's tusk (one hunter remembers the curl
of his dead child) as they pass through a dwindling brake
—its gray twigs turned like spokes of an ignited wheel—
to an etched hollow, and hard lake, maintaining
a simple tree, with limbs fringe-white
above and black below, suitable for hanging,
as the pack, all prinked and singing,
swerves to a call.

Fur bristling,
their quarry holds at a bush,
compact, his collar bell
still tinkling, trying with a paw
to shake it off—too late!—
They are leaping the last hedge, crying—
as he goes, in a flash, abstract,
his eyes blown white.

Rondo

Let me sit in a gray room,
a room empty and breathless

and you talking to me
until I cannot hear you

who are become a thin spiral
of dust, a presentiment

of fine plaster sifting
at angles, at closer congress

to my anger and lust.
Let me sit for a long time

in this sector, if need be
let it be endless

attending a mute
and higher incandescence

of rafters, where joist
and stud and buttress join,

and waiting, if only to guess
what may be assumed

from this, what may release
your spinning light

column of dust; or say
it is too late for your face

to look back on this room
and the least prayer inspire.

Van Gogh: "Starry Night"

Such high, improvident swirls
of ball on yellow ball
of light unwhirling still,
the aspiring town below—
belie his having to descend,
fiercely, into the coal pit,
his coming out
fiercer, to paint the light
behind things: the artist's room,
the tree's irregular bloom.
Nor can it tell
how at the end,
brought to a field of straw
(what is the sun but rings?)
even then he saw
the light behind things.

1962

Bells

Spaces around them, encasing; the way
the clappers fall, and soft tufted sallies;
untumbled, are like banked flames,
suck air from belfries, or seem
to have drunk some darkness vast and friendly,
informal and old . . . Religious
is too strong and musical too weak
for the change-ringings tolled out over our solitude

in nominals that toss or brood,
sounding the right place, the right time.
This is America. I have never been
obsessed with bells;
but for bellringers of small English villages
they are like architecture, kinship, food.

Notes

In spring a child sits down
at the open window to play.
Five lines: black daddy longlegs
dangling, jangling there without
beauty, he could cry.
Spring at my city window.
The child won't go away.

Suite

The table folded west
today, the painting back
above it, armchair two-points-south
below the turned settee: holding
this short, affectionate arc.

Often she moves our things around
and around;
she does not lose any of them,
not a one disappears
or goes unsound.

Table lamp, ashtray, scrap basket, books
and vases by degrees are in it,
casting their little score against
the black; and she
       will ask *is it more*
       attractive is it more
convenient now? For a minute

the old way
sits in my eye, like a negative:
This is the new way.
Soon it will be the old way.
It is the way we live.

Perhaps if I concentrate
around one article
and could describe it perfectly—
its declination, pitch,
its character and pole,

and from this whirling allotropy
arrest one part—
perhaps that moment I
would know what is real,
what tears at her heart.

Fable

The curious woods turned out for him;
and huddled undersize
in a pine tree at the west room
a winter owl (its eyes
an absolute delirium)
blinks as the old man dies.

Attending him there was a girl
who did not minister.
She drifted in the outer hall
like snow-wind in the fir
and let the animals on call
return to what they were.

Bread

There are many ways to live. Whole wheat
is tasty, so are rye and white

and sesame, oatmeal, acorn, maize,
bread tanning forever on trays

of dawn—in factories
and towns, on farms at first light,

even the settled hermit waking
breaks it again, this common thing.

As for me, I'd say one loaf
a day could be enough:

bread for your morning visit, bread
and honey, or bread with tea and marmalade.

Let nobody go wanting, and let the grain
be fresh and broken by the moving sun.

Postscript

Bells go. A gathering in fall
   beside our old grape arbor,
in a falling dusk already cool
   to me as the outsider,

with pointed shoulders quietly
   were in a circle standing,
arrived afar, in hats with brims
   inscrutable and kindly.

And all of this was faint and gray
   like a stencil run too often,
when suddenly the lowering, small
   makeshift cedar coffin

hemorrhaged—as if from empty
   o's dark ink was oozing,
now finally accepted by
   the crusty earth in closing:

and relieved and oddly unattached
   they turned together bowing,
the sun was flowing up the sky,
   the wild little green grapes growing.

TWO:
Shaker Village

The locale of this gathering of poems is an old Shaker village in Massachusetts. The speakers are two children of different centuries, one child a Shaker, the other not.

In 1922, soon after the Shakers vacated the village, one of their houses was transferred to Fruitlands, the nearby museum grounds, where it now displays their tools, recipes, and furniture.

> *These turnings of delight,*
> *roped off, extend a will*
> *to see a versatile*
> *cure for the world's blight*
>
> *in singleness: to see*
> *in a spare and alien*
> *order, even*
> *here, variety.*

The Girl
(c. 1850)

i: Genesis

Craftily it spoke
and, as everything fell
into place, was seen
(they say) to disappear,
subtle and quick,
behind the evergreen,
its blood-berry and song,
and there to coil
like a sundial—

making us wrong
simply in being here?

ii: The Millennial Laws

From chaos, first, came word
of time; and out of the jaws
of time came our good Lord
and the Millennial Laws.

He is our very cause.
And while, with the others here,
I shake and dance—it is
"contrary to order" for

Believers to rest the feet
on the rounds of chairs,
or, ascending, to put
the left foot first on stairs;

to offer the world greeting;
to have right and left shoes;
or, when going to meeting,
not to walk on toes.

To nickname; to mix any
seed with another seed;
to keep a beast for fancy,
or lie curled in bed.

Or own watches; in the halls
to go blinking or yawning;
to tell nonsensical tales.
And there is no returning.

iii: Half-Song

Lord, protect our tender grapes,
and watch the Bible on my shelf;
note my charity and hopes.

The tiger lilies, burning gaps
along the wall, wait like a wolf—
Lord, protect the tender grapes.

Hands are nothing more than cups
to catch the sunlight for itself:
note my charity and hopes.

As I wander by the crops
I feel a frightening, small gulf.
(Lord, protect the tender grapes.)

Unplanted, I repeat in loops:
the seed is split and views itself.
Note my charity and hopes.

Can this be loneliness? Perhaps.
It is, if only I myself
(O Lord) protect the tender grapes,
note my charity and hopes.

iv: Walking Home

Just yesterday, in passing by the water,
we saw a spotted snake, its life in order,
slipping between the reeds, out of our way,
and screamed: to see how surely a snake works
on our very brookside, how its scales are dark
and shiny, and each eye a tiny world.

I have walked here alone. It makes a world
of difference to sit down and build a water-
wheel of some twigs and branches, in the dark
of the old stone bridge—sitting alone in order
that no one can know the wheel is here and works
by itself at night, under the Milky Way.

We like to think ours is the only way,
this formal separation from the world.
We pray, and shake, and learn to do good works,
and I pick herbs and berries, bake, and water
the animals—but like the fruits I order
in boxes, do I lie changing in the dark?

Little by little, I see myself as dark,
intelligent and pretty, measured that way,
too "contumacious" for the Children's Order
that tucks me in—oh, such a tidy world.
Seeing the April blossoms, my eyes water
just for the sake of anything that works.

Nobody shakes and dances, prays or works
harder than I myself, although at dark
I lie awake and wonder: if Holy water
won't take on me, perhaps the "primrose way,"
whatever that can be, for all the world,
is merrier than these winters we keep by order.

Someday let's take off shoes and stockings, order
our frocks by the willow where the brook works
with light unbraided currents into the world.
We'll keep our village elders in the dark
if suddenly our temperate wills give way
to floating palm-leaf bonnets over water:

White boats in racing order, each a world
of violet and dark fern, our handiwork
may carry wayside flowers to bright water.

The Boy
(c. 1950)

i: Shadow Box

And in these days of unbroken fall
of apples and the ripe smell of cider
leaning deep into the cricket grasses
minutes out of Shaker Village,
we park our blue convertible
on our side of the tracks. And wait.
We are too early often. Maybe
my brother in his skullcap haircut
fidgets between my mother and me.
And I take in the windy branchline
going both ways, the stationhouse
of flat maroon, and platform shadows
boxing with little groups of shadow.
Far away the yellow hills.
Happily I think we have
a right to sit here, wait here as
we have to, in the September husk
of light suspended, wondering later
will I remember at the crossing
how the depot's dusty ferns looked down,
poking for their shape in the dust,
while I sat reciting

> *I am the smoke nettle*
> *neutral, without name,*
> *I am chimney pots, a petal,*
> *I am the blue flame*

until we'd see him through the glass,
the steamy tooting 6:05
swerving him (friendly) home again
to a shuttle of bells, steam, shadow, wind,
clouds, and the long day's intelligence.

ii: Fruitlands

> Blankets and Comfortables should be of a modest
> color, not checked, striped, or flowered . . . One
> rocking chair in a room is sufficient . . . Believers
> should not keep any beast that needs an extravagant
> portion of whipping or beating, but such had better
> be sold to the children of this world, or killed. . . .
>   —from the Millennial Laws, 1821

"So when a Shaker died," our guide
explains, "they put him in a pine
unpainted coffin, sometimes with
only initials, age and date
on a small marker facing west,
in simple rows. . . ."
                    A room brightened
as if by skylight—somehow a faint
pinwheel attraction floating over
us. And how to move in this?
No people left, no animal
or mouse, nothing alive at all!
And if they never wanted babies,
why that little cradle there?
How long since the last gathering
in song and dance we hear about,
meetings when a whole community
went shaking into the small hours?
Many questions I don't ask.
The light swallows jangle outside
to the day's undoing, as we go round
and round the inventions of an old
order—a circular saw, the first
flat brooms and metal pens, a palm-
leaf bonnet loom, and common clothespin,
left to the children of this world.

iii: Changeling: Child and the World

Once the infected night
is good—moonless and blank,
empty of parents it seemed
imperative to kill.
Outside, a loping brood
cycles haphazardly, and flocks,
dark in a zero air,
describe the planet's path
and things elliptical.

Under the counterpane
I note the regular
return of singleness:
tonight the little cat
is sleeping, tail in mouth.

iv: Asthma

Miss Perkins, "lady of the bones,"
came weekly with her diagrams
and pointer and left-over bones
(wearing thin silver spectacle rims)
to show my mother how to relax.
Though she looked retiring and feeble,
in the library she would fix
my mother on a sheeted table.
Spring. And the shaken little cherry
tree at our fence was all ahop
in song, and bloom was customary,
a sneezy air over our back stoop
and terrace, like the dust of women.
After my mother, she took me.
She'd gather an engrossing group
of pictures from her wooden box,
and several human vertebrae,
and as I lay out supine, say:
"Think of your head as a balloon
or something light, as if the rest
of you is simply hanging down—
that's the relaxing way to walk,
for then we never need pull back
the shoulders, or push out the chest."
She'd poke her fingers in each crack,
and slowly I became resigned
to thinking this was permanent
until my mother lost her mind
and had to leave us—then she went.
Unlike my mother, who returned.

v: Two in the Oak

The queens are dead:
we play a black-and-white
offense, elbows on knees,
where the leaves rustle away,
holding our own high teas
up in the reddening boughs.

Below the planks our father,
dozing under the *News*,
sways as his hammock sways.

vi: In Time of Harvest

Turning in my window on its thin thread,
a prism puts out pricks
of rainbow-light around my walls and bed.
Are we going somewhere? In the flux
our flowers run to seed,

fraying us into history: on a piece
of yard my father tills
at dusk, unready waves of changes pass
over his garden's witty parallels,
each summer blooming less.

While each particular harvest withers,
up the road our enemy
Mr. Bean, with his little daughters,
lifts golden wheat up to the sky.
And the redhead daughter's caught my eye.

vii: Tiger Lilies

Always earth holds another
forgiveness at its center:
and tiger lilies splinter

cold air for their own colors,
like teeth or smooth young shoulders,
or the ears that tradewinds bother.

viii: Tradewinds

Now a traveler sees
   the local show
of chairs and recipes
   you kept, and how

sweetly a song runs through
   these fragrant ponds
and orchards, where you knew
   the first bonds.

Only an owl (the sly
   neighbor) keeps
an elm comfortably
   tonight: he sleeps

apart, in branches near
   your chosen graveyard,
or wakes to an austere
   silence—tired

and curious sentinel,
   like a lone cross,
working to distill
   some old loss.

One may envy
   that beautifully false
neutrality;
   but when she calls,

a nesting whippoorwill
   allows that it
was only natural,
   your dying out.

Croquet Lover at the Dinner Table
(at a Writers' Conference)

She passes muffins, orders the most remote
and sudden relishes, comments on
the one particular poem you meant to keep
entirely undiscussed, or interrupts
your train of silence with a stab
of curiosity on what you plan
to do next year if love or money won't
come through, as if it were a game
to find you out: to slam you out of court,
to rout the field, dislodge the set-up shot,
provoke your aim, suggest a change of rules
until you feel immeasurably behind
because her eyes are never wicketed,
dead on nobody and poison to the last.

Passion of Crows

Crows never say much. Maybe an old
one years ago stared at the sun
so long its feathers coaled,
and now they cruise for bits of windblown
silver, odd bits of gold,
whatever glints. When we lay down
young in the forest, we heard their noise.
I held you. I meant to explain
how much I—the words caught down
in my throat—a crow shot from the pine
to look for a little blood on the pineneedles.
And here, I think, began my long decline
into inarticulateness,
it is the crows' and mine.

Slow Motion

Nets of morning glories
waiting inland, uphill.
We never went to pick,
only to count blue petals
opening on a wall,
growing haphazardly
awake beside her misty
garden. Year by year
how many morning glories
have walked down to the sea
filling their blue nets?
While the sea got bluer yet.
Grandmother and small boy,
we'd amble up from the shore
at daybreak—her hand
more practical and queer
than my mother's or father's.
And each trip went differently:
one dawn beside her I
could feel her on my other
side as well, and halfway
heard her voice calling
as if to pull us through
some tiny blue archway
suddenly dressed alike
in blue, without goodbye
to anyone, and floating
off in the earliest blue.

Loss of the Unicorn
(reincarnated as wood turtle)

Undercover and feeling his
    forgotten spike,
no longer really caring
    what things are like,

our unicorn stays hard
    to capture, even
if girls feel up to it.
    Some turtle-haven!—

A sticky terrible wind
    had raised the wood
to such a pitch, he headed
    out for good,

tiles scrubbed, in character:
    dingy-proud
and overserious, like
    a small black cloud.

And crawled to a nearby well
    circled with stone
to find a late narcissus,
    petals turned in.

Before the Prophet

I

In the Dark Section with Her Sisters

"We had gathered, broken and returned
so many times, with our baskets of flowers,
to the leaf-shadowed square, while
he who loved us
lay sick in a high window,
that by now we could hardly remember
how once the air brimmed with invisible wings,
high flutterings the length of our yellow city
over market and fountain, its ribbon of water.
Now dawn silhouetted
only a cynical eastern skyline,
a look of migrations, the streets cleared
and watered for circulation
of trotting carriages from the far stone gates,
and ourselves there, waiting
his cure, and tied for
him to the streets' cold constructions,
where the bells sent over turrets
and pinnacles their recurrent
'No . . . No . . .' until watchmen paced
with lanterns of the evening.

"Soon a frost was dusting the courtyard, the pale chestnut:
and from the hill's high terraced windows
rich ivy looped its fingers,
and our hands were cold.
The city had us, huddled
and bootless, keeping our stations
for a few coins, our baskets full
of poppies, carnations, marigolds,
like piping coals.

And when news came
that he who had promised us golden sunsets
and the glowing windows of other homes
waiting across the bay, was dead—hawks broke,
a black drumbeat, from the citadel."

II
Water Faces: with her sisters on a bridge

On this still, green evening,
the pink road
interrupted by a bridge,
you may recall uncertain vertiguous
faces you have seen, on a word or a look,
swirl suddenly inward or away,
a retrograde whirling, like drainwater leaving.
Across the bridge sits the old black tree,
or whatever it is, from here only
opaque and overhanging, riding down
to make, again, that part of the water black.
A full moon hangs off in a corner
and reflects.
                    Four on a bridge, at the railing:
four idle girls just older than waifs,
who have come through that period . . . One wears
a yellow hat. They wait in dresses blue,
green, red, and gray. This last,
the nearest, looks our way
(the others gaze the other) but her face
is blank, is simply missing.

The sky, the whole landscape, twists
    without moving.

III
Hope after Sunset: her child

Then at the bole of night
behind that tree, a staining
spiral of fire stroked her a child:
delivered also at night,
by cruel division.

And coming through
necessary weeds, she knelt alone
at the riverbank to set
her very light child,
muffled to his ears
in a tight-woven basket of no worth,
seaward like a hollow pulse.
And down the floating stream he goes
by plainsong or moonpull. He won't,
he can't remember how he came

to where the sun bobs, the scenery, the clouds
    and sky do,
and what's beneath him tilting,
and banks becoming flowers,
flowers, through a circuit
of blond dawns, whose water birds
once fluttered and were left behind,
tracing their deep rotation.

Marks: after Edward Thomas

Somewhere in a dream
the house I left, unsatisfied,
as bidden by the warm
cross breezes, another May's
words in a sheaf tied,

somehow I know winter is there
now, the furze, charlock
and dwarf gorse carried to snow, its white
brief covering, nor
am I there quite,

instead squirrel, sparrow,
and rabbit will shadow or dent
the snow and oversee
my empty house, hearing
at dusk, beyond dusk, a tapping inside.

And they'll say of my dim
machine there, its keys
are tapping to release by the narrow
fireplace leaf after leaf
of an old discrepancy

while, ever reticent,
they creep in—those small
enough to slip through the knothole—
where finally the drifted papers
say what I meant

to say, or was finally meant to be,
and my animals draw close
to read. The field mouse shudders.
In that solitude
they strike a soundless frieze.

The Glassblower
(for Plato)

His, too, is a clear study
against the least crystal,
or seed, keeping the stress and fragrance
of a blackbird floating in the rain
like a prime number,
or a Mondrian,

or a clove—its small
and formal kindling on the tongue.
He works in winter, loving
children not his own

who, at the fair,
may see his orange liquor pale
and snake to an amazed bubble to conjure
a vase, a flower,

      and take from there
a sudden little ecstasy, a fear.

Note on Henry VIII

When Henry's deluge hit the roof
no alibi was waterproof.

He went over the heads of many
to prove, as happily as any,

that cleanliness can have its use.
Unluckily he did produce

Elizabeth, the Virgin Queen,
the saddest masochist we've seen.

To a Young Lady at the Museum

Considering life, for once, in terms of art
I remember what a teacher said to me
(quoting Aristotle, I believe)
that the possible improbability
is less acceptable, in art, than the
probable impossibility.

That is to say: babies have been known
to tumble seven stories to the ground
without sustaining any injury
beyond a minor shakedown.
Just the other day
I read of one who tumbled seven stories
and landed in a neighbor's yard without
a fracture, falling with the unconcern
of one intoxicated (which, as it
later developed, his father was, and in
a rage had thrown him out the window).
But this was so unlikely an occurrence
that no one would believe it in a play.

But take that curious painting by Paul Klee
of Sinbad battling a hostile water,
how strange it seems, how wonderful it is,
a spear too long for one his size to handle,
a boat too small to keep a man afloat,
three variously decorated fishes,
open-jawed but ever held at bay,
flatly emerging from the shades of blue.
No one questions the authenticity.

And oh young lady, barely out of school,
now passing to the outer gallery,
having gazed awhile on Sinbad's critical danger
as if it didn't apply: how can you feel
in this current turn of nights and days
that one day you will die?

A Romantic Angel

Society and songs
he fell from—lakes
of light, and rings,
and by the twilight spokes

of sheltering umbrellas: he flew
in the better circles
there, at his debut,
a cocky socialite: or else

resting, his tucked wings folded, while
above, for guardians,
like bells,
hung identical little talismans

to allay what jelly-spooks
hovered about his covers
perspectiveless, awake
and whispering, "You are in others . . ."

He dreamed another planet
plain as fact
so very long with nothing on it,
until like a mere hat rack

aslant and visionary,
from the dust all curved and wan,
up shivered a lime tree—
yes, with a few pale leaves and coal-black stem

buttoned with limes, at once
to furl like a hieroglyph
into a tuned silence
of air, where it slept.

Country Matters

I'm tired of your saying no
you won't get in this hammock with me.
Day's over, dear. We've let the lazy
whitethroat clear his throat and go,
dusk go, and Taurus reappear.
On such a deep blue evening, Zeus
himself as a great snorting bull
came down: the continuity
of all mankind's suggested here.
No worry that we'll drain the sky
in my hammock hung from spruce to spruce,
or a new continent beget.
And yet—your ankles and your wrists,
are they too delicate to know?
The elements of evening sigh
for us, that want you in my net.

Jumping

My feet come down
on the soft blue carpet

jumping, not
a rigmarole

I want to repeat,
my personal rope goes

up and down,
I must suppose

I'm more adroit
nowadays than when

under the sun
this way and that

I swung in the trees,
or earlier lay flat

on a rock to the moon,
all shadow and silhouette

turning my thin
profile

to the tideglaze—
where in the dross

of deep sea-glossaries
the tingling wan

fishes spun out
their destinies

going up and down.
Oh, I think of it,

I marvel at what
colors I've won,

battles I've fought,
since I came in

touching the wheel.
Yes, I was smart

to anticipate
the galaxies,

to be there in
the bursting grain

of love, or light,
or whatever it was,

hearing the night-
long whirls of cloven

stars, black holes, spinnars
that flash and doze

in dots of braille
away, uncurl

a universe
of stone afloat

like tapestries
unwinding. All

this wasn't news
to me, of course,

who had the beat
already, the will

to work and rise
(jump forty-nine!)

and socialize.
Of course I hate

my jumping chart,
it's hard to feel

at ease in a ripple
of entropies

running on down
the shadowcone

of years and years,
but any feat

is possible,
and I'll retain

the leaf and tendril
sleeping in the brain,

the lost starfish, its frail
and perfect dawn

that makes me twirl
about, to get

my jumping done,
our curtains shut

as usual,
I jump hirsute

among the sun
and other stars.

At Home

"He sailed upon the seas and waited . . ."

Those lotuses are my daughters' water wings
floating promiscuously in the pool we bought
from the beaming one-eyed salesman, who only saw
pools in a panic vision, lacking perspective.
Our daughters bob and float, tied to their moons,
until no longer lotuses they, one
by one, run in to you to change.
And while I go on paying by installments
and breezes warm the leaning maple trees,
our pool reflects its hospitality.
Some afternoons a poolless neighbor girl,
after a few noteworthy dives and flounces,
dangles her small, crossed ankles in the water.
I am half-tired, I think, of musing on
her mythological significance.
I let the seasons go—they float
away and back again, as I unwind
at my uprooted beach umbrella, with
a second-rate old fashioned, home too soon
from some essential trip I haven't taken.
I see the downtown twinkle. The pool puts on
its wasting little shades in replica
empty of travelers, as dusk unloads
flowers, puppies. When I head in for supper
I am too easily identified,
the table full of voices, where I stay,
liking the loom you ravel and unravel.

Willow Street

Not far from here it bends, slightly, like tomorrow.
The houses along it, dusk-colored, are mostly square.
Guilt, being only a secret sorrow
over something lost, is not there.

Not far from here, it has no waterfall
or failing wood—
all things returned we still
look forward to, long afterward.

Here the odd, off-center log shifts
and arranges, as stockings depend
innocently again on the hearth, and the drift
will not change from the intended, or end.

Ars Poetica

It is fall. A brook sounds past our window,
and against our window the plucked
apple tree is a measure . . .
House and garden, form and content.

Barring the moonlight,
a circular clotheshorse in the yard
wears articles no longer
orange and white and green:
like notes we forgot to bring in, they hang
in a manner of speaking, and have their music.
They sing our separate hungers.
And these scruffy old-family acres
hold what the land once was.
Inside, at my pop-and-flutter
kerosine lamp, alone I am writing
words, a fluting of bones,
a place for trapping the quick light into
shapes that gesture,
until any sheer figure at all can be
emblematic, a blue stone.

   I like sitting here among stones—
folded deep into the night, hearing
our nightly brook, drawn back
to the scored things I need to know.